KICKING YOUR HOLIDAY STRESS HABITS

To:

From:

WITHDRAWN

for Phil and Andy
our holiday energizers

Kicking Your Holiday Stress Habits

Tips for avoiding seasonal stress and enjoying holiday treasures

NANCY LOVING TUBESING, EdD
DONALD A. TUBESING, MDiv, PhD

Pfeifer-Hamilton Publishers
a division of Whole Person Associates Inc
210 West Michigan
Duluth MN 55802-1908
218-727-0500

Kicking Your Holiday Stress Habits

©1996 by Nancy Loving Tubesing and Donald A. Tubesing

Printed in the United States of America
10 9 8 7 6

ISBN 1-57025-096-0

Whether you're celebrating St. Nicholas Eve, Kwanza, Winter Solstice, Navidades, Hanukkah, Christmas, St. Lucia Day, Boxing Day, or New Year's, holidays are intrinsically stressful.

This book is a holiday gift to you—an opportunity to reflect each year on what stress you want to eliminate and what stress you want to savor. Enjoy the process!

You'll find lots of questions in these pages—with a few examples to stimulate your thinking. We hope they lead you to answers that help you avoid holiday stress traps and savor the treasures of the season.

★ Do you look forward to the holidays with excitement and enthusiasm?

★ Are the holidays a time of spiritual centering and meaning for you?

★ Do you find your creative juices flowing as you anticipate gift-giving?

★ Are your holidays usually enriched by meaningful contact with family and friends near and far?

Terrific! This book should help you affirm your positive stress habits and identify why they're so energizing for you.

WHAT IS HOLIDAY STRESS?

★ Is your holiday season filled with "shoulds" that don't bring the fulfillment you yearn for?

★ Do you feel guilty when it seems that others are enjoying the holidays more than you?

★ Do you find yourself overindulging, overscheduling, overspending and still not feeling satisfied?

★ Do you end the holidays feeling more empty than you did at the beginning?

If so, you're probably trapped in some negative holiday stress habits. This book is designed to help you identify your patterns, discover more positive alternatives, and plan for more satisfying and meaningful holidays this year.

WHAT IS HOLIDAY STRESS?

Holidays are occasions for celebration.

They offer opportunities for personal reflection, participating in tradition, gathering with family, connecting with friends, gift-giving, spiritual renewal—all potential sources of joy and satisfaction.

WHAT IS HOLIDAY STRESS?

Holidays may also cause problems.

Family tensions, overcrowded social schedules, painful memories of lost loved ones, an endless list of tasks to accomplish, and unfulfilled expectations can rudely intrude on the mind and heart—leaving us feeling overwhelmed and depressed.

WHAT IS HOLIDAY STRESS?

Let's face it. The holidays are usually marked by profound conflicting emotions. We feel exhilarated. We feel despondent. We feel irritated then filled with love. We feel anxious and peaceful. We feel expectant then disappointed. Even when the holidays seem "perfect" and go exactly as planned, the increased tempo and stimulation may be draining. It's no wonder we need time to "recover" from the holidays.

WHAT IS HOLIDAY STRESS?

What feelings do you associate with the holidays?

enthusiasm, worry

WHAT IS HOLIDAY STRESS?

Kicking your holiday stress habits doesn't mean getting rid of all your stress. Who would want to? Stress can be a turn-on. It can pump you up, give you energy, supply zest and excitement. We all need the stimulation of positive stress.

But stress can also wear you down—sapping your energy. Unfortunately the holidays are often characterized by this type of negative stress.

WHAT IS HOLIDAY STRESS?

Think back to the holidays last year:
What do you recall as your special holiday "turn-ons"?
(positive stress habits)

   caroling party, midnight mass, skiing, family time

What do you remember as your particular "wear-outs"?
(negative holiday stress habits)

   last minute gift-making, staying up too late,
   open houses

WHAT IS HOLIDAY STRESS?

You may have noticed that the same events and situations that arouse positive stress reactions can also provoke negative stress reactions—depending on the proportions and our attitudes.

Fortunately we are in control of both of these dynamics. Baking cookies is a delightful and energizing holiday activity. Baking twenty varieties of cookies all by yourself at the last minute or when you resent the time or the role is a sure set-up for distress.

Positive stress or negative stress—we decide. The accumulation of attitude and proportion choices we make over the holiday season and over the years shape our holiday stress habits. Consider six typical holiday stresses that could be traps or treasures—depending on your attitudes and actions.

WHAT IS HOLIDAY STRESS?

Holiday trap or treasure? The choice is yours!

★ Santa Claus Trap or Santa Claus Treasure?
  The stress of giving and receiving.

★ Activity Trap or Activity Treasure?
  The stress of time and energy management.

★ Tradition Trap or Tradition Treasure?
  The stress of finding meaning.

★ Life Script Trap or Life Script Treasure?
  The stress of familiar patterns.

★ Magic Trap or Magic Treasure?
  The stress of expectations.

★ New Leaf Trap or New Leaf Treasure?
  The stress of resolutions for change.

HOLIDAY TRAP OR HOLIDAY TREASURE?

Santa Claus Trap

The child in each of us is fascinated with the giving/ receiving aspect of the holidays. We are greedy. We are afraid we won't get what we want. We want everything and can't set priorities. We give away what we wish to receive. We try to please others with our gifts. We confuse the gift or the cost of the gift or the number of gifts with the love and concern we really wish to give or receive.

SANTA CLAUS TRAP

Santa Claus Treasure

Everyone loves gifts—both giving them and receiving them. Holidays offer the opportunity to cultivate the attitude of gratitude and to indulge our most altruistic urges. Gift-giving is a marvelous outlet for our creative urges—from the planning, to the shopping and making, to the wrapping and tagging. Delightful!

SANTA CLAUS TREASURE

How vulnerable are you to falling into the Santa Claus
Trap?

1 10
not at all   extremely

What giving/receiving habits could get you into trouble
this holiday season?

trying to find "perfect" gift, wanting too much

SANTA CLAUS TRAP

In what ways does gift-giving and receiving energize your holiday season?

Fun to surprise people, feel appreciated

SANTA CLAUS TREASURE

Activity Trap

One of the dangers of the holiday season is losing control of the activity calendar. Some of us never say no and crowd our days and nights with parties, plays, and other social "obligations" as well as the holiday preparations. Overwhelming!

Others sit home waiting for the phone to ring with an invitation. Underwhelming!

How much we must do during the holidays—shopping, cookies, cards, decorations, gifts, entertaining, travel, music!

How much must we, really?

ACTIVITY TRAP

Activity Treasure

There's something intrinsically satisfying about a busy schedule, especially at holiday time. The hustle and bustle fills us with a sense of purpose and worth. The intense holiday pace also helps us appreciate, by contrast, the moments of solitude and silence. Social gatherings reconnect us with our support network.

ACTIVITY TREASURE

How likely are you to get caught in the Activity Trap?

1 10
not at all   extremely

Where is your schedule:
overwhelming?

traveling to see both families

underwhelming?

nothing special for New Year's

ACTIVITY TRAP

How does the hustle and bustle of the holiday season
intensify your pleasure?

love to be busy, makes the season special,
sacrifice work for pleasure

ACTIVITY TREASURE

Tradition Trap

We cling tenaciously to the rituals and traditions of the past. What happens when partners' backgrounds or preferences differ? Usually folks take on at least some of the new without relinquishing any of the old. What a burden! Sometimes we perpetuate a tradition that has lost its meaning or its appropriateness.

What happens when death or distance or changing life circumstances disrupt our celebration patterns?

TRADITION TRAP

Tradition Treasure

Holidays are a time for getting in touch with the sources of meaning in our lives. The rituals and traditions that characterize our celebrations can stimulate spiritual reflection and centering as well as a sense of playfulness, excitement, or wonder.

Traditions often help us get through the difficult times when our feelings don't quite match the occasion.

TRADITION TREASURE

To what degree is the Tradition Trap one of your holiday stress habits?

1 10
not at all   extremely

What rituals/traditions do you need:

to change?

include outsiders

to invent?

holiday fast

to surrender?

rich foods

to resurrect?

writing letters

TRADITION TRAP

What holiday traditions are most meaningful for you?
Messiah concert, popcorn balls, making photo collage

TRADITION TREASURE

Life Script Trap

Holidays draw us inevitably back into old feelings and roles remembered from childhood or from the years of child-rearing. We try to recreate the "magic." We try to avoid the remembered pain.

As we gather together with our families we find ourselves slipping unconsciously into our relationship habits, thrust back into needs and expectations of earlier years that may no longer be appropriate.

LIFE SCRIPT TRAP

Life Script Treasure

No matter what our age, the holidays give us permission to be childlike, imbuing the festivities with magic and meaning. We can bring the past into the present, luxuriate in the comfort of familiar sights and sounds and activities.

As the family gathers together we can celebrate our heritage and affirm the love that connects the generations, no matter how much we grow and change.

LIFE SCRIPT TREASURE

To what extent do you feel trapped in roles from your
Life Script during the holidays?

1 10
not at all   extremely

What events particularly trigger your regression?

playing Santa Claus, arguments

LIFE SCRIPT TRAP

As you celebrate your heritage during the holidays, what memories, activities, and relationships do you particularly cherish?

lighting the candles, connection to faith community

LIFE SCRIPT TREASURE

Magic Trap

The myth of the "perfect holidays" permeates our preparations. We feel let down when reality doesn't match our Madison Avenue expectations.

Not only do we look for magic in our activities, we even expect ourselves to feel a certain way during the holidays (Peaceful? Loving? Joyous?) and are disconcerted when we feel lonely, sad, angry, or discouraged instead of "happy."

MAGIC TRAP

Magic Treasure

Anticipation. Excitement. High hopes. Holidays are full of magic. The child within us cherishes the promise implicit in hanging decorations, the smell of special food, the full mailbox, the visit to cousins, the possibility that wishes may come true.

Holidays offer an opportunity to feel deeply—to experience pain, elation, love, disappointment, loneliness, impatience, joy, anxiety, peace—to be touched to our core.

MAGIC TREASURE

How vunerable are you to feeling disappointed when holiday expectations aren't met?

1 10

not at all   extremely

In what ways are you likely to fall into the Magic Trap?

trying to make it perfect for everyone

MAGIC TRAP

How do your feelings and expectations enrich the
holidays for you?

enjoy planning for gifts all year long

MAGIC TREASURE

New Leaf Trap

Too often we turn New Year's Day into a day of personal reckoning, "shoulding" ourselves with all the large and small ways we don't measure up to some internal or external yardstick.

Wallowing in remorse, guilt, and self-recrimination, we resolve to clean up our act—to quit smoking, to lose weight, to balance the checkbook, to be more patient with our kids or parents, to write more letters, to exercise regularly, to watch less TV, to curtail our spending habits.

Unfortunately, we usually set a totally unrealistic agenda for self-improvement that is doomed for failure.

NEW LEAF TRAP

New Leaf Treasure

Turning the calendar to a new year does offer a natural opportunity to reflect on the year past and plan for the year to come!

Remembering the highlights and the low points of the year brings new perspective. Celebrating projects accomplished, progress toward goals, life storms weathered, and opportunities seized gives us courage to step into the new year with confidence. Savoring connections with family and friends allows us to know that we are loved and accepted.

Every new page on the calendar reminds us that we can begin again, making whatever small changes will enrich our lives and the lives of those around us.

NEW LEAF TREASURE

How likely are you to fall into the trap of trying to turn over too many new leaves?

1 10

not at all   extremely

What unrealistic resolutions do you make nearly every new year?

lose 10 pounds, no charge cards, stop drinking

NEW LEAF **TRAP**

As you think over the past year:
What experiences are particularly memorable?

Mike's suicide, refinishing woodwork, peace workshop

How have you been strengthened and supported?

more faith, learned new skills, broadened horizons

What one or two changes would you like to make during the year ahead?

more playtime, find a walking buddy and DO IT!

NEW LEAF TREASURE

Your holiday preparation agenda resembles the space shuttle prelaunch checklist. Holiday trap or holiday treasure? It's up to you!

You could put on your martyr's cloak and try to fulfill your grandiose expectations in suffering silence.

You could work your fingers to the bone cleaning and sewing and cooking and wrapping and writing and orchestrating and pleasing others.

HOLIDAY TRAP OR TREASURE?

OR you could take this opportunity to relinquish your stranglehold on the holidays, inviting others to share in the burden (and benefit) of getting ready.

OR you could assemble the clan for some values clarification, polling family members about what they really treasure about the holidays, then making a plan that includes everyone.

OR you could decide that this is the year for some kind of alternative celebration.

HOLIDAY TRAP OR TREASURE?

You've just moved to a new city and are going to be separated from your family during the holidays this year. Holiday trap or holiday treasure? It's up to you!

You could pine away for them, focusing on the pain of the separation and your disappointment because it just can't be Christmas without the kids (or the grandparents).

HOLIDAY TRAP OR TREASURE?

OR you could see this as an opportunity to build your support network by inviting friends or acquaintances to share your celebration.

OR you could brainstorm creative alternatives for making contact with the far-flung family. A conference call? A round robin letter? A "memory box" with symbols of what you cherish about one another? A videotape of affirmations and memories? A progressive audiotape?

The possibilities are limitless!

HOLIDAY TRAP OR TREASURE?

Since the same situation can provoke a variety of responses, what motivates us to choose a holiday trap rather than a holiday treasure? You might be surprised to discover that both your valued positive stress habits and those pesky negative ones stem from your belief system—your views about yourself, the world, and what makes life worthwhile.

If one of your deeply held values is the worth of work above all else ("idle hands are the devil's workshop"), it's no wonder you run yourself ragged during the holidays. If you grew up believing there would never be enough to satisfy you, don't be surprised at your lack of enthusiasm for gift-giving or your overindulgence in treats.

If you really want to kick your holiday stress habits, you'll need to get in touch with what's really important to you.

HOLIDAY TRAP OR TREASURE?

Once you've identified what's really important, you'll be free to unleash your creative energy on finding less stressful ways to satisfy those underlying needs.

Ask yourself three questions:

- What's of major importance to me?
- How do I hope to accomplish it?
- If that doesn't work, how else could I meet the need—or what would be a satisfactory substitute?

Having a big party may not be the best way to touch base with old friends. If sharing and caring is of prime importance to you, a quiet evening in front of the fire might be your first choice. Hand-crafted gifts are not the only way to demonstrate your uniqueness. If your time and energy are at low ebb, you could devise clever name tags instead.

HOLIDAY TRAP OR TREASURE?

What five ingredients are essential for your holiday to be meaningful? Be specific!

hand-made gifts, traditional foods, family gathering, big party, spiritual renewal

1.

2.

3.

4.

5.

HOLIDAY TRAP OR TREASURE?

What do these ingredients indicate is of major importance to you this holiday season?

unique, personalized giving; connecting to the past; fun, playfulness; self-reflection and peace

HOLIDAY TRAP OR TREASURE?

Know what "goodies" will fill you.

What kind of contact will be fulfilling for you? What kind of gift exchange will be meaningful to you? What do you need to help your heart and soul feel refreshed?

★ If you know clearly what you want, it is easier to choose activities that are likely to satisfy your desires.

★ As an evolving human being, your needs are constantly changing. Don't assume that what filled you last year or a decade ago will be satisfying this season.

TIPS FOR KICKING HOLIDAY STRESS

Ask for what you want.

Don't hint. Don't wait for someone to read your mind. Don't expect others to guess what will satisfy you. Speak up.

* If you're lonely, ask someone to share your celebration—or ask to share in someone else's.

* If you love surprises, let people know.

* If you need time alone in the midst of togetherness, say so.

A HELPFUL HINT: if you can't get what you want, want what you get; it's much more satisfying than wishing for the impossible.

TIPS FOR KICKING HOLIDAY STRESS

Give yourself permission to feel.

Listen to yourself. Embrace your feelings. Pay attention to your inner messages.

★ Feel what you feel, not what you "think you are supposed to feel," or "wish you felt." When you feel down, feel down. It won't last forever. When you feel excited, go ahead and enjoy it.

★ Trying to manipulate your feelings, or act contrary to them, will distance you from yourself.

TIPS FOR KICKING HOLIDAY STRESS

KICKING YOUR HOLIDAY STRESS HABITS

Select celebration patterns with care.

Remember your past and bring it to the present. Your "treasure box of memories" will contain pain as well as warmth and joy but it offers you a personalized source of depth and richness.

★ Resurrect a tradition from your childhood.

★ Create new traditions that fit your present time in life.

★ Ask others about their rituals, pick one that's new for you, and try it as well.

TIPS FOR KICKING HOLIDAY STRESS

Set priorities.

List all the things you want to accomplish before/during the holidays. Cross out unnecessary activities.

⭑ Refuse to suffer. Do unpleasant tasks as quickly and painlessly as possible, then reward yourself.

⭑ Keep for yourself the activities you enjoy, even if they aren't essential or could be done by others. You need them. They nurture you.

TIPS FOR KICKING HOLIDAY STRESS

Turn obligations into energizers.

Even exciting tasks, repeated year after year, may turn into obligations. Creatively update the tasks so they provide new energy.

* If your holiday card list conjures up an image of drudgery, write a compliment to each friend rather than a history of the past year.

* Surprise selected people on your list (not just close friends) with a brief long distance phone call.

* Pack up your cards and do the job at the library or a favorite restaurant.

* Any new approach can energize you.

TIPS FOR KICKING HOLIDAY STRESS

Make positive contact with others.

Holidays give us natural opportunities to connect with the spirit and gifts of the folks around us.

* At a party make sure you have a good conversation with several people. If parties aren't your bag, make contact in some other situation (at church? on the commuter train? at the laundromat? with a classmate? with a neglected friend or neighbor?).

* If your friend or family list is disturbingly short, look around for others in the same boat. Try Meals on Wheels, the crisis shelter, local hospitals, a halfway house, homes for the elderly, etc. Someone in your community needs your love: reach out and touch someone—for both your sakes.

TIPS FOR KICKING HOLIDAY STRESS

Give meaningful gifts.

Give presents (buy or make something) and give your presence (pledge your time and attention).

* Don't just give tickets to a cultural or sports event—plan to go along and share the experience together.

* Give a gift of words: affirmations, memories, thanks.

* Give blood. Give groceries to the food shelf. Give a mother with toddlers an afternoon of child care. Give new books to your school library. Give a hand to a neighbor in need.

* Don't forget to put yourself on the gift list. Treat yourself to a gift that's just perfect for you.

Take care of yourself.

Don't over-eat, over-drink, over-party—these celebration habits sap your vitality and diminish your ability to participate fully in the holidays.

★ Protect your physical energy. Learn to celebrate without abusing your body.

★ During this high intensity season, allow space for rejuvenation. Get plenty of sleep, recharge your batteries with regular exercise, and take time out every day for relaxation.

TIPS FOR KICKING HOLIDAY STRESS

Laugh.

augh a little or a lot, depending on your level of stress. Laughter reduces tension and provides perspective.

★ Do something unusual and outrageous each day. If you're not sure what to do, consult a child!

★ Tickle your funny bone often with cartoons, jokes, songs, stories, movies, clowning around. Invite your family, friends, and coworkers to join in the process.

★ Practice seeing the humor in all your holiday dilemmas.

TIPS FOR KICKING HOLIDAY STRESS

Pay attention to your spirit.

Holidays invite reflection. Nurture this opportunity as part of your celebration. Take time to sit down by the side of the road and let your soul catch up with you.

⋆ In the midst of the hustle and bustle of the holidays, listen to your core. Touch it. Allow it to touch you. What do you believe? What are your roots? What's really important to you?

⋆ Light a candle every evening. Focus on the flickering flame and allow your thoughts and prayers to rise shimmering upwards into the silence.

TIPS FOR KICKING HOLIDAY STRESS

How about you? Do your holiday stress habits help you cherish holiday treasures or lead you into holiday traps?

How do you hope this year will be different?

slower pace, more meaning, fewer "shoulds"

What are you most concerned about this holiday season?

PLANS FOR KICKING HOLIDAY STRESS

What holiday stress habits do I want to "kick" this year?

disappointment/suffering habit

Which energizing strategies would maximize my
positive holiday stress and minimize my negative
holiday stress?

ask for what I want

How and when could I use them?

family meeting to coordinate plans/responsibilities,
post wish list on fridge

PLANS FOR KICKING HOLIDAY STRESS

My plan

This year I will:

PLANS FOR KICKING HOLIDAY STRESS

This book comes to an end—but it's really a beginning. We've helped you design a strategy for kicking your holiday stress habits. Now it's up to you to implement your plan.

Breaking habits isn't easy. New behaviors and attitudes feel awkward for a while. Change is usually uncomfortable as well as stimulating. Go ahead and take the risk! Experiment. Tamper with tradition. Try something new. Treat yourself to a more meaning-full and satisfying holiday.

PLANS FOR KICKING HOLIDAY STRESS

Authors of **The Caring Question, Seeking Your Healthy Balance,** and the YMCA's **Ys Way to Stress Management,** the Tubesings have been pioneers in advocating an interdisciplinary approach to stress management and wellness. This holiday stress book is patterned after Don's best-selling classic, **Kicking Your Stress Habits.**

If you found the holiday reflection process helpful, you might enjoy other products available from Whole Person Associates, the stress and wellness specialists. Call us for information on our workshops-in-a-book, unusual relaxation tapes, video courses, and teaching resources for educators and group leaders.

Call toll free: 800-247-6789.

Kicking Your Holiday Stress Habits is available in quantities for your corporate promotional or gift-giving needs.

MEET THE AUTHORS